FEAR IN BATTLE

W9-BVP-944

AMS PRESS
NEW YORK

FEAR IN BATTLE

By JOHN DOLLARD, PH.D.
Research Associate in
Social Anthropology (Professor)

With the Assistance of

DONALD HORTON, PH.D.
Research Assistant in Anthropology

The Institute of Human Relations
Yale University

WASHINGTON
THE INFANTRY JOURNAL
1944

Library of Congress Cataloging in Publication Data

Dollard, John, 1900-
    Fear in battle.

    Reprint of the 1st rev. ed. published in 1944 by the
Infantry journal, Washington, in series: Fighting forces
series.
    1. Fear. 2. Psychology, Military. 3. Courage.
I. Horton, Donald, 1910- joint author. II. Title.
III. Series: Fighting forces series.
U22.3.D64   1976   355.4'01'9   75-41076
ISBN 0-404-14714-3

Reprinted from the edition of 1944, Washington, D. C.
First AMS edition published in 1976
Manufactured in the United States of America

AMS PRESS INC.
NEW YORK, N.Y.

TABLE OF CONTENTS

ACKNOWLEDGMENTS

This study of fear and courage under battle conditions is indebted first of all to 300 veterans of the Abraham Lincoln Brigade, each of whom spent at least five hours completing an arduous questionnaire; to Yale University and the Rockefeller Foundation who have severally provided administrative and financial aid; and to many unnamed friends who have helped by discussion and action. This research has not been sponsored by the War Department, but the work has been done in the hope that the results would prove to have military value.

THE GROUP—
300 VETERAN SOLDIERS

When this study was begun 18 months ago battle-wise riflemen were hard to find. The dive-bomber, the blitz, and the modern tank have changed conditions so much since 1918 that experiences of World War veterans could hardly be very helpful. The research therefore sought men who had had experience under modern combat conditions and found the men of the Abraham Lincoln Brigade—Americans who volunteered for service in the Civil War in Spain—ready to coöperate. Their participation in the research cost them much time and labor, generously given.

This group varied as to age, region, social status and political conviction. They had in common the belief that by volunteering they were fighting for democracy. Different as they may have been from a cross-section of the American Army, their experience made hardened soldiers of them all, and soldiers, in whatever army, have much in common. As the conditions of battle are similar, so the men who fight wars learn the same lessons. The testimony of these men seems sensible and soldierly.

The typical informant was a rifleman, noncommissioned, poorly trained by American Army standards, wounded. All observers seem to agree that he was a tough fighting man.

This study bears only on the military experience of the informants and is not a canvass of their political views.

THE FINDINGS IN BRIEF

1. Fear is useful to the soldier when it drives him to learn better in training and to act sensibly in battle.

2. The commonest symptoms of fear were: pounding heart and rapid pulse, tenseness of muscles, sinking feelings, dryness of mouth and throat, trembling, sweating. Involuntary elimination occurred infrequently.

3. Seven out of ten men reported experiencing fear when going into first action.

4. Fear is greatest just before action.

5. Sixty-four men out of a hundred agreed that they became less afraid the more times they went into action.

6. Fear "of being a coward" diminished rapidly after the first action.

7. Wounds most feared were those in abdomen, eyes, brain and genitals.

8. Enemy weapons most feared were bombs, mortar shells, artillery shells, bayonet and knife, and expanding bullets.

9. Fear of bombs centered in the sound of the bomb dropping and on the concussion of the exploding bomb.

10. The presence of hunger, thirst, fatigue, ignorance of plans, idleness increases the danger from fear.

11. Eight out of ten men say it is better to admit fear and discuss it openly *before* battle.

12. Seventy-five out of one hundred believe that all signs of fear should be controlled—*in battle.*

13. Experienced men who crack up should be treated leniently, deserters shot, and green men made to stay and face the music.

14. The most important factors in controlling fear are: devotion to cause, leadership, training and matériel.

15. Only one man in four thought that feelings of fatalism or belief in luck were of much importance in bearing fear.

16. Veteran soldiers learn that to be busy means to be less afraid: "When fear is strong, keep your mind on the job at hand."

17. Thinking that the enemy is just as scared as you are is helpful in controlling fear.

18. Eight out of ten men believe that hatred is important to the effective soldier—but hatred of the enemy's cause, not of him personally.

19. Fear may stimulate a soldier to fight harder and better, if danger to the self also suggests danger to the outfit or cause.

20. The best discipline is based on the willing acceptance of orders by purposeful and instructed men.

PART I: SOME FACTS ABOUT FEAR

Fear is a strong drive, and it is learned. Fear is a normal response to danger. In some situations and degrees it is useful; in others, dangerous.

FEAR IS NORMAL

Fear is a normal experience in battle. Experienced men admit it and are not ashamed. Seventy-four per cent of our informants reported they were afraid in first action. Many seem to have been afraid in later actions as well.

Fear, though a strong response, need not determine behavior. Eighty-five per cent said that there was an occasion when they were very scared but went ahead anyhow.

Fear is useful in that it makes men cautious when under fire. The line between a hero and a reckless man is often a fine one. But fear can lead to over-caution. Fifty-nine per cent of the veterans stated that there were occasions when they were too cautious and had their efficiency reduced by fear.

Even a moment of panic is not exceptional. Sixty-one per cent of the informants "lost their heads for a moment, couldn't control themselves and were useless as soldiers for a little while."

It seems a fair inference that men should feel no shame at sensing fear within themselves. No man need think that "he's the only one to be afraid."

[4]

ONLY A FEW MEN WERE UNAFRAID . . .

. . . when first going into action

QUESTION. . . "Did you experience fear
when going into your first action?"

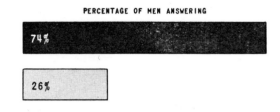

PERCENTAGE OF MEN ANSWERING

EXPERIENCED FEAR   74%

DID NOT
EXPERIENCE FEAR   26%

AND MANY CONTINUED TO EXPERIENCE

FEAR when going into subsequent actions

QUESTION. . . "If you were in more than
one action, did you experience fear when
going into later actions?"§

PERCENTAGE ANSWERING

ALWAYS AFRAID   36%

SOMETIMES AFRAID   55%

NEVER AFRAID   9%

§The chart is based on the answers of only those men who were in more than one action.

FEAR IS USEFUL IN TRAINING

Fear is a drive which incites to action. The action which follows on fear may be profitable or useless from the military standpoint.

Fear may be aroused in training so as to serve a useful purpose. It can motivate men to learn those habits which will reduce danger in battle.

Our informants are unanimous in thinking it important to have a veteran soldier explain to the men in training the protective value of the things they are learning. Proper motivation is important in any learning process and fear is a strong motive if it is working on the right side.

In order to understand the value of training, the men should visualize the situation in which the training is to be used. For this reason, apparently, our informants stress the value of giving the trainees a real picture of the dangers of battle. Our informants, who suffered many casualties in early actions as a result of poor training, are all the more keenly aware of the importance of careful preparation.

It is apparent from reports in current journals that American training authorities are taking proper advantage of the fear motive.

FORESIGHT OF DANGER can serve . . .

. . . to MOTIVATE LEARNING

Our informants say that as a technique of training. . . . GIVING A MAN A REAL PICTURE OF THE DANGERS OF BATTLE will tend to make him a better soldier.

PERCENTAGE OF MEN WHO SAY IT WILL MAKE HIM. . .

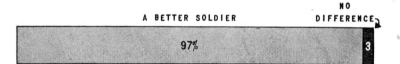

A BETTER SOLDIER   NO DIFFERENCE

97%   3

. . . and HAVING A VETERAN SOLDIER EXPLAIN TO THE MEN on the basis of his personal experience THE LIFE-SAVING IM-PORTANCE OF THE THINGS THEY ARE LEARNING . . . tends to make them better soldiers.

PERCENTAGE OF MEN WHO SAY THIS TRAINING-TECHNIQUE
WILL HAVE THE EFFECT OF MAKING A MAN. . .

A BETTER SOLDIER   NO DIFFERENCE

99%

FEAR COMES MOST OFTEN
BEFORE THE BATTLE

Men differ in the timing of their fear. Nearly three-quarters (71 per cent) of the veterans report feeling fear more often just before battle; 15 per cent during battle; and 14 per cent after the action is past.

QUESTION. . . "In general did you experience fear more often just before going into action, during the action, or after the action?"

PERCENTAGE ANSWERING

EXPERIENCED FEAR MORE OFTEN. . .

. . . BEFORE GOING INTO ACTION | 71%

. . . DURING THE ACTION | 15%

. . . AFTER THE ACTION | 14%

[8]

REASONS FOR FEAR
IN THREE PHASES OF ACTION

The comments of the men were studied to find the reasons given for experiencing fear at a particular time. They report:

REASONS FOR FEAR BEFORE ACTION

"Because of not knowing what to expect."

"When you lay around waiting for something to happen you may worry."

"Because of the terrific image of warfare drilled into me by years of training, I was much more afraid before I went into action."

REASONS FOR FEAR DURING ACTION

"This depends on how active you were. If inactive, more fear."

"The most intense fear is during a hot action where the soldier is not occupied such as under bombardment or shelling."

"I was wounded and lay between the opposing lines for a number of hours. The fear of a counterattack and being helpless was very great."

"Especially in retreat."

REASONS FOR FEAR AFTER ACTION

"The thoughts of risks taken were regarded with fear upon reflection."

"The let-down from tenseness usually found me wilting."

"Though consciously I ceased to fear, I did have nightmares for a long time after."

SYMPTOMS OF FEAR IN BATTLE

Many men think that "fear is in the mind." This is an error. Fear begins with strong bodily responses and is then registered in the mind.

If men are to learn to control fear, they must recognize its commonest symptoms.

The most frequent signal of fear in battle, according to our witnesses, is a pounding heart. Paired in frequency of occurrence are strong feelings of muscle tenseness and a "sinking feeling in the stomach."

In a third group of lesser frequency three symptoms appear: dry mouth, trembling, and "clammy hands."

Feeling faint is much more common than actually fainting.

Involuntary defecation or urination, the legendary signs of battle-fear in the novice, are comparatively rare.

FEAR BEGINS for most men . . .
. . . WITH A POUNDING HEART
BUT FEAR SHOWS ITSELF IN MANY OTHER FORMS

Our veterans were asked to check the symptoms of fear they experienced in battle. This is how they answered. . .

FEAR SYMPTOM	PERCENTAGE OF MEN WHO EXPERIENCED THIS SYMPTOM
Pounding heart and rapid pulse	69%
Strong feeling of muscular tenseness	45%
Sinking feeling in the stomach	44%
Dryness of mouth and throat	33%
Trembling	25%
Sweating of palms of hands	22%
"Nervous" perspiration ("cold sweat")	18%
Loss of appetite	17%
Prickling sensation of scalp and back	17%
Feeling faint or weak	14%
Feeling slightly sick at the stomach	14%
Roaring or ringing sensation in ears	8%
Involuntary urination	6%
Involuntary defecation	5%
Vomiting	less than 1%
Fainting	less than 1%

The percentages total more than 100%, since informants usually marked several symptoms.

FEAR OF WOUNDS

Greatest fear is aroused by the prospect of wounds in the abdomen, eyes, brain, and genitals.

Despite the propaganda of childhood, there seems to be little fear of being "shot through the heart."

The dangerous abdominal wounds, which take many lives, are properly feared. Puncturing the lining of the gut releases a virulent flood of infection into the body.

Fear of loss of sight is a dread of that fumbling darkness in which a man is cut off from the signs and signals of security and direction.

Men value their brains as the symbol of personality itself. Thoughts of damage to the brain raise fear of a life aimless, helpless and uncoördinated.

A man's sense of his manliness and integrity is based in part on the possession of genital power. Thus, damage to genitals is one of his most ancient and deep-rooted fears.

If it can be shown that the wounds most feared are in fact not the most common ones, much reassurance might be provided by this fact.

WOUNDS IN THE ABDOMEN
ARE MOST WIDELY FEARED

QUESTION. . . "Did you have a special fear of being wounded in certain parts of the body?"

VETERANS WHO HAD A SPECIAL
FEAR OF BEING WOUNDED. . .

PERCENTAGE OF MEN ANSWERING §

. . . IN THE ABDOMEN   29%

EYES   27%

BRAIN   22%

GENITALS   20%

LEGS
AND FEET   12%

HANDS
AND ARMS   12%

FACE   7%

TORSO
(INCL. CHEST,
HEART, LUNGS)   6%

. . . But 22% of the men did not fear one wound more than another.

§ The total percentage is more than 100 since a number of men mentioned more than one part of the body.

MOST-FEARED WOUNDS

Feared weapons and projectiles are divided into three groups. At the head of the list is bomb shrapnel.

Next in a group of four are trench mortar, artillery shells, bayonet and knife, and expanding bullets.

The lowest group in point of fear-arousing power includes grenades, strafing, machine gun, tank and dive-bomber.

A weapon may be high on the list either because it is especially common and dangerous, perhaps the case with artillery shells, or because something about it arouses irrational fear, perhaps the case with air-bombing. The machine gun should probably be high on the list because it is actually dangerous, but the men may feel that, though dangerous, it is in the realm of the familiar and that they know how to cope with it.

If a list of "most-dangerous weapons," determined by the number of the casualties they cause, could be compared with a list of "most-feared weapons" one could discover the weapons which though relatively less dangerous are yet high on the fear list. For the latter some prophylactic measures against fear might be devised.

WOUNDS INFLICTED BY BOMB SHRAPNEL ARE MOST WIDELY FEARED

QUESTION. . . "Were there certain weapons
or projectiles that you had special fear
of being wounded by?"

FEAR OF BEING WOUNDED BY . . .

PERCENTAGE OF MEN ANSWERING §

. . . BOMB SHRAPNEL   36%

TRENCH MORTAR   22%

ARTILLERY SHELLS   18%

BAYONET AND KNIFE   16%

EXPANDING BULLETS   16%

GRENADES   6%

OTHERS   13%
(STRAFING, MACHINE GUN
BULLETS, TANKS, ETC.)

. . . But 16% of the men did not fear one weapon more than another.

§ The total percentage is more than 100%, since several men mentioned more than one
weapon.

FEAR OF BOMBS

When danger is near, the sights and sounds connected with it acquire the power to arouse fear. A great majority of men react strongly to the *sounds* of bombing, *i.e.,* to the sounds of dropping bombs, to the noise and concussion of the exploding bombs. Only 8 per cent of the men found the sight of dropping bombs or seeing the damage caused by bombing more terrifying.

The longer the dropping bomb is heard, the more frightening it becomes. Fifty-six per cent of the men expressed this opinion, while only 17 per cent thought "hearing the bomb for a short time before it hit" more frightening. The rest were neutral.

The men further expressed the view that being bombed in a city is more frightening than being bombed at the front but that day-bombing and night-bombing are about equally fear-inspiring. Planes circling before dropping bombs are more feared than planes which appear and drop bombs suddenly.

If there is no defense against bombing, 82 per cent of the men felt that "firing back at the plane with your rifle" has a good effect on morale. The reasons may be that firing a rifle is reassuring because it is so often effective in other situations, and that "doing something" takes attention off fear.

THE SOUNDS ARE MOST TERRIFYING . . .

To four out of ten men . . . SOUND OF BOMBS FALLING
To three out of ten men. . . SOUND AND CONCUSSION OF EXPLOSIONS
To one out of ten men . . . SOUND OF THE BOMBING PLANES

The men were asked to rate their fear of different aspects of bombing. They answered as follows:

MORE FRIGHTENED BY. . .

PERCENTAGE OF MEN ANSWERING

. . . SOUND OF BOMBS FALLING 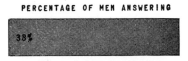 38%

. . . SOUND AND CONCUSSION
OF BOMBS EXPLODING  33%

. . . SOUND OF PLANES 11%

. . . SIGHT OF BOMBS FALLING 5%

. . . SIGHT OF BOMB-DAMAGE 3

NO DIFFERENCE 10%

PART II: CHANGES IN FEAR

Fear should be rationed . . . only enough to make men careful . . . not enough to make them panicky. Fears change under battle conditions but some fear must be borne.

SOME BATTLE FEARS CHANGE, OTHERS DON'T

The men were asked to rank certain typical fears of soldiers for first and later actions in order to see whether these fears change over a period of time.

For instance, the fear "that you might turn out to be a coward" apparently dies out in veteran soldiers. Thirty-six per cent give it first place as a fear in first action, but only 8 per cent give it first place in later actions. The man who has done well in a number of actions obviously loses his fear that he will crack in the next one.

On the other hand, veterans seem to be somewhat more afraid of "being crippled and disfigured for life." Only 25 per cent rank this fear first in early actions, while 39 per cent give it first place in later actions. It may be that the veteran acquires a more literal idea of the damage caused by severe wounds. Fear of *pain* of wounds and fear of being killed do not change between first and later actions.

Fear of being captured and tortured was a real fear with many of these men. The horrors of civil war are well known; and the International troops were bitterly resented by their enemies. Fear of torture seemed to increase among veterans, since 19 per cent of them feared it as compared with 8 per cent of newer men. The Japanese may be attempting to arouse just such a fear among our men at the present time.

[18]

MEN RATE THEIR FEARS DIFFERENTLY AS GREEN TROOPS AND AS VETERANS

The informants were asked to say which of five common fears they experienced most strongly when going into their first action and which was their strongest fear after they became veteran soldiers.

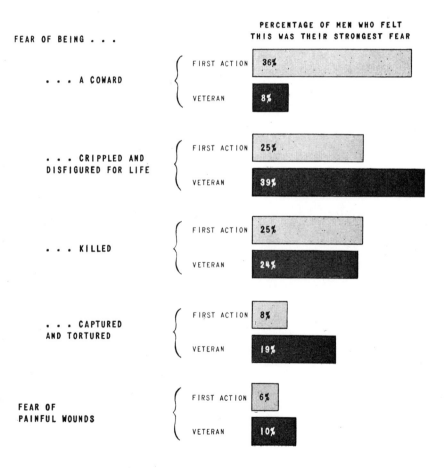

PERCENTAGE OF MEN WHO FELT THIS WAS THEIR STRONGEST FEAR

FEAR OF BEING . . .

. . . A COWARD
FIRST ACTION 36%
VETERAN 8%

. . . CRIPPLED AND DISFIGURED FOR LIFE
FIRST ACTION 25%
VETERAN 39%

. . . KILLED
FIRST ACTION 25%
VETERAN 24%

. . . CAPTURED AND TORTURED
FIRST ACTION 8%
VETERAN 19%

FEAR OF PAINFUL WOUNDS
FIRST ACTION 6%
VETERAN 10%

FEARS THAT DIDN'T PAN OUT

When the civilian looks forward to battle his fears are a composite derived from childhood training, war novels, enemy propaganda, the movies and many other sources. Some of these fears persist, others fade under the impact of battle conditions.

When asked to name the lively fears which diminished in actual combat the men give first a group of five, all of about equal frequency. The real significance of these responses lies in the total list of fears rather than in their order of frequency. Apparently some men learn that airplanes are not so dangerous to combat troops as they are advertised to be. Artillery fire—the rain of shells—also tends to lose some, though of course not all, of its frightening power.

In popular imagination the classic test of the soldier has been "going over the top." Fifteen per cent of the men found it easier to meet this test than they had supposed. Perhaps the great physical strain of advance under combat conditions tends to take the soldier's mind off fear.

The sight and cries of the wounded, the sight of blood, the presence of dying and dead men are all experiences strange to civilian life. Soldiers sometimes adapt to such sights and sounds better than they thought possible.

They find that such sights, however ghastly, do not injure a man except in his mind.

As already shown, "fear of cowardice" drops out rapidly as men become veterans.

BATTLE DANGERS can be EXAGGERATED

QUESTION. . . "What was the most striking example of a
thing you expected to fear in battle only to find that it
did not bother you in actual combat?"

**EXPECTED TO FEAR BUT ACTUALLY
NOT BOTHERED BY. . .**

PERCENTAGE OF MEN ANSWERING§

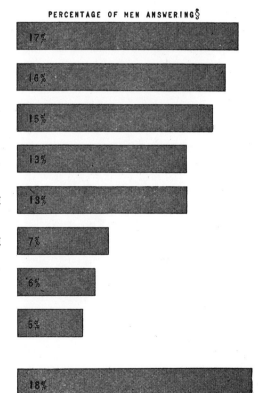

. . . PLANES — 17%

. . . ARTILLERY — 16%

. . . GOING OVER THE TOP — 15%

. . . THE SIGHT OF DEATH — 13%

. . . ONE'S OWN COWARDICE — 13%

. . . THE NOISE OF BATTLE — 7%

. . . NIGHT ACTIONS — 6%

. . . TANKS — 5%

. . . OTHER DANGERS — 18%

§The percentages total more than 100%, since some men mentioned fears in more than one
category.

BATTLE-WISE MEN
ARE LESS FEARFUL

In the absence of evidence, opinions might easily differ concerning the degree of fear experienced in repeated actions.

Our informants actually do differ as might be expected. The majority, 64 per cent, feel that men become less afraid the more times they go into action. Their comments seem to indicate two reasons for this lessening of fear. First, the men have been exposed to danger before and have survived; why not again? When they have been afraid, but found themselves unhurt, their fear response tends to drop out. Secondly, they learn better how to protect themselves and thus indirectly reduce the degree of danger to which they are exposed.

Fourteen per cent feel that men tend to be more afraid the more times they go into action. The implied reason for this answer seems to be that some men wear out nervously, *i.e.,* are unable to sustain their reactions against fear; such a let-down of anti-fear defenses might occur where men were exposed to an unusual variety of morbid sights or narrow escapes. Perhaps, also, wounded men, knowing the full reality of pain, tend to become more afraid in subsequent actions.

A third group, 22 per cent, noticed no difference in fear during repeated action. It may be that for them the opposing forces creating and reducing fear tended to balance.

[22]

QUESTION . . . Do men become more afraid or less afraid, the more times they go into action?

ANSWER:

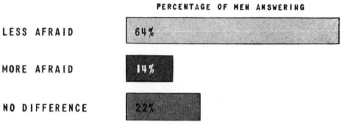

PERCENTAGE OF MEN ANSWERING

LESS AFRAID	64%
MORE AFRAID	14%
NO DIFFERENCE	22%

COMMENTS FROM THE MEN . . .

. . . which explain differences in opinion

WHY LESS AFRAID

"Most feel less afraid, especially if they come out of battle unscathed."

"The more I knew how to protect myself, the less afraid I was."

"You develop confidence in yourself and gradually lose fear."

"When a soldier continuously goes into many actions, he becomes less afraid."

"With experience, get used to it."

WHY MORE AFRAID

"Their nerves get shot."

"Fear that chances of survival diminish with each action."

"By stages men get more afraid--as different types of death become evident--men get more scared of all those different ways of getting killed and maimed."

"Especially those wounded."

"The thought that--'This is my time'--increases with each succeeding action."

PART III: TECHNIQUES OF FEAR CONTROL

Men can learn to control fear. Keep your eye on the job, they say. Don't *brood on it.* Do *anticipate it, discuss it openly.*

RECOGNIZE FEAR EARLY

A man may recognize fear only when it is extreme, as in a panic reaction.

If he has waited that long, he has waited too long. If the first signals of fear are noticed, control responses can go into action immediately. Here lies the importance of knowing the common, bodily reactions which register fear.

The man who knows he will be afraid and tries to get ready for it makes a better soldier. Fifty-eight per cent of the men share this opinion.

Similarly, 98 per cent of our veterans say that planning in advance to meet the possible dangers of battle is useful. In this case fear leads the man to canvass danger situations and often to work out ways of meeting them.

The men seem to want to be warned of approaching danger so they can get ready for it. Forty-nine per cent say that men are more afraid when told suddenly they are going to attack, while only 27 per cent believe that being warned in advance of attack makes men more afraid.

The men prefer to volunteer for a dangerous mission. Fifty-five per cent say that going on such a mission in obedience to orders makes men more afraid, while only 28 per cent believe that "making up your own mind" to undertake it makes men more afraid. Evidently when men make up their own minds they can prepare themselves for fear, calculate the risks and advantages and thus behave more steadily.

[24]

WHEN PANIC STARTS . . .

. . . it's TOO LATE

Six out of ten veterans believe that a man who EX-
PECTS TO BE AFRAID IN BATTLE AND TRIES TO GET READY
FOR IT makes a good fighter.

PERCENTAGE OF INFORMANTS WHO THINK SUCH A MAN WILL BE

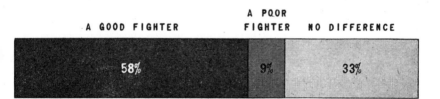

A GOOD FIGHTER	A POOR FIGHTER	NO DIFFERENCE
58%	9%	33%

Most veterans believe that HAVING PLANNED IN ADVANCE
HOW TO MEET POSSIBLE DANGERS IN BATTLE makes a man a
BETTER SOLDIER.

PERCENTAGE OF INFORMANTS WHO THINK THAT HAVING PLANNED
IN ADVANCE TO MEET DANGER MAKES A MAN

A BETTER SOLDIER	NO DIFFERENCE
98%	2

FEAR SHOULD BE DISCUSSED—
BEFORE BATTLE

It is not enough to know passively that other men are afraid or to know the common symptoms of fear. Fear should be brought into the open and discussed.

Eighty-four per cent of our informants vote for the open recognition and discussion of fear. In comments they state that such discussion reduces fear, helps to avoid feelings of guilt at being afraid and makes the frightened man feel less of a "special case."

The soldier feels better knit into his group when he knows that others are afraid. He does not expect to be scorned because he is afraid himself. Seventy per cent of the men found it helpful to be told that others were afraid, too.

A lesser number, 58 per cent, found it useful to admit their own fear to another man. If such an admission is treated in a friendly way the "fear of being afraid" is reduced.

Such an open discussion of fear might come best from a battle-tested man who could stress not only *that* he was afraid but *how* he dealt with his fear and went ahead in spite of it.

MOST MEN FAVOR DISCUSSION OF FEAR

QUESTION. . . "What is your opinion on the question of having open discussion among the men on the subject of fear?"

PERCENTAGE OF MEN ANSWERING

FAVOR DISCUSSION 84%

OPPOSE DISCUSSION 16%

KNOWING HE IS NOT THE ONLY ONE
AFRAID makes a man a BETTER SOLDIER

QUESTION. . ."What was the effect on your behavior of having some-one let you know that the other men were scared too -- that you weren't the only one?"

PERCENTAGE ANSWERING

A MUCH BETTER SOLDIER. 27%

A SOMEWHAT BETTER SOLDIER. 43%

NO EFFECT. 24%

A POOR SOLDIER 6%

FEAR SHOULD BE SUPPRESSED— IN BATTLE

Seventy-five per cent of the men say that signs of fear should be suppressed in battle. However freely fear is discussed before battle, however afraid a man may be, he must avoid *acting* afraid under battle conditions.

They cite the fact that expressions of fear tend to excite similar behavior in others. The sight of a frightened man tends to distract a fellow-soldier from his job of fighting.

But they stress also that coolness is contagious. Ninety-four per cent of the men feel they fought better after observing other men behaving calmly in a dangerous situation.

In the same vein, our informants testify to the tonic effect of high morale in an outfit. Soldiers coming into such a group feel it at once. Ninety-seven per cent of the men agree to the proposition that "knowing the morale of your outfit is high" makes better soldiers.

Even those who vote negatively on the score of suppressing signs of fear in battle do so reluctantly. They explain that fear is reflex, unwitting, that control of it may not be possible, but they grant it is important in every case to try.

[28]

FEAR CAN BE CONTAGIOUS . . .

Seven out of ten veterans believe that signs of fear should be suppressed
in battle.

QUESTION. . . "Do you think that it is important
for soldiers not to show signs of fear in actual
battle?"

Signs of fear. . .   PERCENTAGE OF MEN ANSWERING

'SHOULD BE SUPPRESSED   75%

NEED NOT BE SUPPRESSED   21%

NO OPINION   4

. . . and COURAGE CAN BE CONTAGIOUS

The men were asked:

"What was the effect on your behavior of observing other men acting calmly in a dangerous situation?"

                                        PERCENTAGE ANSWERING

It made me. . .

    . . . A MUCH BETTER SOLDIER   69%

    . . . A SOMEWHAT BETTER SOLDIER   25%

        HAD NO EFFECT   6%

DISTRACTION

Fear has work to do. It can make men assiduous in training and careful on the field of battle. When this work is done fear is useless and destructive.

One good way to combat useles fear is to think about something else.

Eighty-four per cent of our veteran informants felt that concentrating on each step of a task when in the presence of danger made them better soldiers.

Concentration on the task provides a distraction from fear and makes men more efficient. When a man stops reacting to danger signals, he is no longer afraid.

Similarly, if the man's attention is fixed on setting a good example when under fire the effect is to make him a better soldier. Ninety-six per cent of our informants share this opinion. Apparently, the man who is setting a good example is less likely to be thinking about the danger to himself.

Even cracking a joke in the face of danger is useful. Seventy-five per cent of the men think a funny remark helps to resist the pressure of a tight spot.

Among other effects, such a remark results in shifting attention from danger signals.

Men who say they are less afraid once action starts explain the fact in the same way. The great exertion required by running and dropping during infiltration tends to preoccupy the mind to the exclusion of fear.

The technique of distraction should work as well for unconscious as for conscious fear.

CONCENTRATION ON TASK . . .

. . . during a battle COUNTERACTS FEAR

Most men found that "concentrating on each task they had to perform in reaching their objective" made them less afraid.

	LESS AFRAID	HAD NO EFFECT
PERCENTAGE OF MEN ANSWERING	84%	16%

A man who TRIES TO SET AN EXAMPLE OF COURAGE tends to become a BETTER SOLDIER

QUESTION. . . "What was the effect on your behavior of trying to set an example of courage for others to follow?"

PERCENTAGE ANSWERING

ANSWER. . .

"MADE ME A MUCH BETTER SOLDIER"   69%

"MADE ME A SOMEWHAT BETTER SOLDIER"   27%

"HAD NO EFFECT"   (4%)

"THE ENEMY IS AFRAID TOO"

Soldiers often build up an image of the enemy as strong, efficient, fear-
less. It does not always occur to them to put themselves in the enemy's
shoes. Once they understand that the enemy is scared too, they take a
real comfort in the idea. Of the men in our sample who had this thought,
72% reported that it made them better soldiers.

QUESTION. . . "What was the effect on your behavior of thinking that
the enemy was just as scared as you were?"

PERCENTAGE OF MEN WHO

HAD THIS THOUGHT   DID NOT HAVE THIS THOUGHT

61%	39%

OF those men who did think the enemy was afraid . .

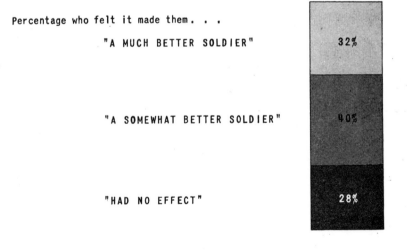

Percentage who felt it made them. . .

"A MUCH BETTER SOLDIER"   32%

"A SOMEWHAT BETTER SOLDIER"   40%

"HAD NO EFFECT"   28%

KNOWING THE ENEMY IS AFRAID GIVES CONFIDENCE

REASONS WHY:

"Made me feel twice as bold and ready to attack immediately"

"This always helped—makes us even"

"I knew the enemy was scared to death and I knew we could take advantage of that fear"

"That gives you a feeling of courage"

"I knew it after I saw some prisoners"

"Felt better to think so"

"It is very good if you can get the enemy to demonstrate that, such as provoking them to fire wildly at night, thinking they are attacked"

"Inform the soldiers that the enemy is human and is just as scared"

BUT SOME DID NOT FIND THIS THOUGHT HELPFUL:

"A consoling thought—nevertheless, I still had fear"

"No difference; we were both scared"

BELIEFS IN LUCK
AND PAINLESS DEATH

The casual gossip of old soldiers has it that beliefs in luck or fatalism play a rôle in controlling fear. Our evidence tends to support this belief but only mildly.

Fifty-eight per cent of the veteran soldiers in our sample never had the feeling that they were lucky and could not get hit. There was too much plain and bitter evidence to the contrary. The 42 per cent who had such thoughts are about evenly divided on the score of the helpfulness of these thoughts. Only about a fourth of the men, therefore, found this notion of help in controlling fear. After all, a man could sustain such a belief only so long as he had not been hit, and 58 per cent of our informants were wounded at least once.

Similarly, there seems to be only limited comfort in the thought that if hit, the soldier would never know the difference. Fifty-nine per cent of the men who had this thought stated that it had "no effect." Thirty-nine per cent thought it was helpful and tended to produce better soldiers. There must have been too much evidence that many wounds do not kill but instead cause severe pain and shock.

Beliefs in luck and painless extinction can play only a modest rôle in combatting fear in experienced soldiers.

"Feeling that you are lucky and can't get hit"
. . . HELPED ONE OUT OF FOUR

QUESTION. . . "What was the effect on your behavior of thinking that you were lucky and could not get hit?"

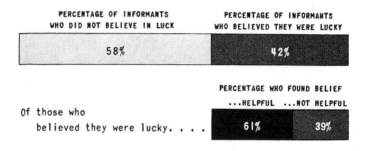

PERCENTAGE OF INFORMANTS WHO DID NOT BELIEVE IN LUCK	PERCENTAGE OF INFORMANTS WHO BELIEVED THEY WERE LUCKY
58%	42%

Of those who believed they were lucky. . . .

PERCENTAGE WHO FOUND BELIEF
...HELPFUL ...NOT HELPFUL
61%   39%

"Thinking that if it hit you, you would never know the difference" . . . HELPED ONE IN FOUR

QUESTION. . . "What was the effect on your behavior of thinking that if it hit you, you would never know the difference?"

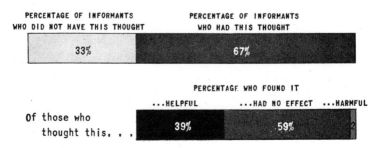

PERCENTAGE OF INFORMANTS WHO DID NOT HAVE THIS THOUGHT	PERCENTAGE OF INFORMANTS WHO HAD THIS THOUGHT
33%	67%

Of those who thought this. . .

PERCENTAGE WHO FOUND IT
...HELPFUL   ...HAD NO EFFECT   ...HARMFUL
39%   59%

HOW TO TREAT
A PANICKY SOLDIER

Men who crack up in battle are a chronic military problem. Our informants have different recommendations for different cases.

They favor leniency for the veteran who fails after going through many actions with a good record. Only 3 per cent would shoot him; 70 per cent favor removing him from the lines. The men indicate in their comments that a soldier may have just about so many battles in him and after he goes through these he should be indulgently treated if he breaks.

The green man who refuses to go over should be made to face the music. Only 8 per cent would have him shot. They recommend informal and verbal coercion of various types with the idea of "giving him a chance," "getting him to try it."

Seventy per cent believe that the chronic deserter should be shot.

It is worth noting that recommendations for psychiatric treatment are not common. The substitute which these men seem to offer is discussing with the man "what he's fighting for," attempting to increase the positive will to fight rather than analyzing fear.

It was apparent in the answers that the veterans advocated doing things in order, *i.e.,* first talking to the man, then shaming, then removal from lines or shooting. There seems to be a set of opinion against the use of violence, with the practical comment "be careful about beating or shooting, because the man has friends and they have guns."

[36]

Veterans say —
SHOOT the chronic deserter

Recommended treatment for man who deserts several times. . .

Remove him from the lines — 21%
Let his squad talk to him — 4
Let him alone — less than 1%
Kid him along — less than 1%
Shame him — 4
Make him stay and face it — 7%
Have him shot — 70%

BE LENIENT with the veteran who cracks up

Recommended treatment for veteran with good record who finally cracks up. . .

Remove him from the lines — 70%
Let his squad talk to him — 25%
Let him alone — 14%
Kid him along — 8%
Shame him — 4%
Make him stay and face it — 3
Have him shot — 3

. . . and with the green man who is afraid

Recommended treatment for green man who refuses to go over. . .

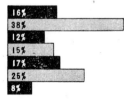

Remove him from the lines — 16%
Let his squad talk to him — 38%
Let him alone — 12%
Kid him along — 15%
Shame him — 17%
Make him stay and face it — 25%
Have him shot — 8%

§The percentages total more than 100, since some men recommended more than one kind of treatment.

PART IV: FEAR AND MORALE

Fear, fused with hunger and fatigue, tends to drive men out of battle. Other stronger forces must be pitted against fear to drive men in. The net balance is morale. . . .

FORCES THAT DRIVE MEN TO QUIT THE BATTLE

Where evil rumors are thick, there a situation of demoralization exists. What are the forces which produce such a situation?

First, of course, *fear* which is ever-present but greater in situations of defeat, retreats and punitive casualties. Fear tends to produce escape responses which take men out of battle.

Then, *ignorance or doubt* about the true state of affairs. Such suspicion tends to reduce the zeal, confidence and expectation of success of the men. Seventy-six per cent stated that "not knowing the objectives of the outfit" made them poorer soldiers.

Hunger and *thirst,* excessive *heat* and *cold,* prolonged *fatigue* all tend to force men out of battle. Hungry men and tired men try to find food and rest at the expense of those acts which make a man efficient in battle. Eighty-three per cent of the men felt that being very tired made them poorer soldiers.

Hostility toward own leaders, periods of waiting with nothing to do, obvious enemy superiority in matériel all play a rôle as forces which drive men out of battle.

These forces tend to add up. When all are present strongly a dangerous situation is created. Destructive rumors arise, and sometimes that breakdown in organization which produces panic and flight. Poor morale is not simply a question of fear but of factors working jointly. The several army services which control hunger, cold and fatigue play a constant morale-building rôle.

[38.]

MAJOR FORCES AGAINST MORALE —
DEFEAT . . . IGNORANCE . . .
DEPRIVATION . . . DISTRUST . . .

The veterans were asked: "What are the most common conditions in which demoralizing rumors are likely to spring up?"

THEIR ANSWER . . .

PERCENTAGE OF MEN ANSWERING §

DEFEATS - RETREATS - HEAVY CASUALTIES	39%
IGNORANCE OF OBJECTIVES - LACK OF RELIABLE NEWS	38%
POOR FOOD - CLOTHING - SHELTER	34%
DISSATISFACTION WITH LEADERSHIP	26%
INACTIVITY AND IDLENESS	26%
EXCESSIVE FATIGUE	21%
TECHNICAL SUPERIORITY OF THE ENEMY	14%
LACK OF SUPPORT BY HOME-FRONT AND REAR	9%

§ Percentages total more than 100%, since many informants mentioned several items.

FORCES AGAINST FEAR—
THE OVER-ALL VIEW

Fear tends to push a man out of battle. It is best controlled by other forces which tend to push him in.

These men believe that devotion to war aims plays a great rôle in controlling fear. If a man knows what he is fighting for, and has an intense personal need to win, his zeal in battle will tend to triumph over his fear.

Like all experienced soldiers, these veterans know the importance of leadership, training and matériel in reducing fear. These sheer organizational factors are among the most potent solvents of fear.

Leadership keeps the soldier's eye on the job at hand. Training sets up strong responses to command which tend to dominate over fear. Matériel provides the means of attack, defense and survival which make it difficult for fear, hunger or other dangerous drives to become strong.

Fear is thus not controlled by mental magic. It is controlled by making other forces stronger than it. The whole organization of an efficient army helps to control fear.

QUESTION . . . "What would you say are the most important things that help a man overcome fear in battle?"

OUR INFORMANTS MENTIONED. . .

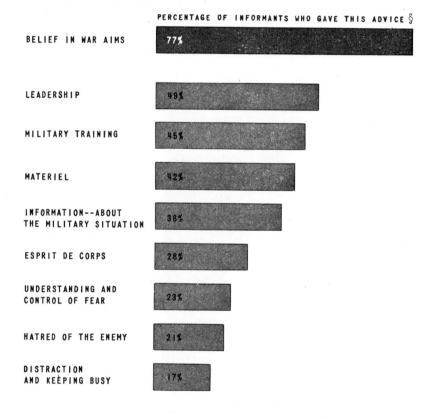

PERCENTAGE OF INFORMANTS WHO GAVE THIS ADVICE §

BELIEF IN WAR AIMS	77%
LEADERSHIP	49%
MILITARY TRAINING	45%
MATERIEL	42%
INFORMATION--ABOUT THE MILITARY SITUATION	38%
ESPRIT DE CORPS	28%
UNDERSTANDING AND CONTROL OF FEAR	23%
HATRED OF THE ENEMY	21%
DISTRACTION AND KEEPING BUSY	17%

§The total percentage is more than 100%, since many of the informants mentioned several items.

Against Fear . . .

IDENTIFICATION WITH CAUSE IS
A POWERFUL ANTIDOTE

War aims, say our informants, must be concrete, personal, intimate. The soldier must have the war aims within his skin, operating as personal motives to fight. It is not enough that statesmen know the cause is just. The soldier must know it and feel it.

All of our informants say that having a clear idea of what is at stake in the war makes a better soldier. All testify to the usefulness of discussing war aims and their importance in the personal lives of the men. All stress the value of thinking that a better world will follow when the war is won. Men fight better when they recoil in imagination from the prospect of the world the enemy intends to create.

The inevitable fear of battle has a powerful opponent in this profound conviction of the justice and importance of cause. The soldier must be able to answer the question "What's in it for me or my group if we win?" He must feel that there is a lot.

But—the soldier in battle is not forever whispering, "My cause, my cause." He is too busy for that. Ideology functions *before* battle, to get the man in; and *after* battle by blocking thoughts of escape.

Identification with cause is like a joker in a deck of cards. It can substitute for any other card. The man who has it can better bear inferior matériel, temporary defeat, weariness or fear.

MEN WHO UNDERSTAND WAR-AIMS ARE BETTER SOLDIERS

IN TRAINING

Discussing the war aims and their importance in the personal lives of the men makes better soldiers in the opinion of most of our veterans.

Those who say discussion of war aims makes a man. .

. . . . . . "A MUCH BETTER SOLDIER"

. . . "A SOMEWHAT BETTER SOLDIER"
Those who say   "IT HAS NO EFFECT" (1%)

93%

6%

IN ACTION

Having a very clear idea of the things that were at stake in the war made them better soldiers.

Those who say a clear idea of the war made them. . .

. . . . . . "A MUCH BETTER SOLDIER"

. . . "A SOMEWHAT BETTER SOLDIER"
Those who say   "IT HAS NO EFFECT" (1%)

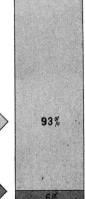

93%

6%

Against fear . . .

LEADERSHIP

It is a military axiom to say that decisive and competent leadership helps to control fear. Our informants place a high value on this factor.

Good leaders are especially valuable in the pinches when danger is great. Eighty-nine per cent of our informants emphasize the importance of getting frequent instructions from leaders when in a tight spot.

All of our men agree that the commander who is admired and respected has better soldiers under his command. The soldier can afford to feel that a commander worthy of respect will take no unnecessary risks with men's lives.

Men like to follow an experienced man. Practically all our informants agree that going into action with a tested man made them better soldiers. Here again the experienced man knows how to accomplish objectives with a minimum of risk. He sets an example of coolness and efficiency which impels similar behavior in others.

The commander can best reward his men by looking after their food, shelter and smaller comforts. Such a leader, by general testimony, incites more soldierly behavior in his men.

The presence of careful and thoughtful leadership builds up a force which helps resist fear.

LEADERSHIP MEANS REASSURANCE

Getting frequent instructions from officers when in a tight spot
makes a man. . .

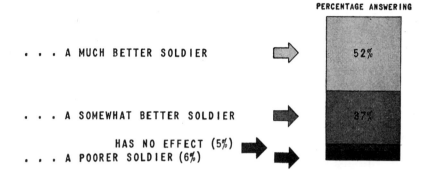

PERCENTAGE ANSWERING

. . . A MUCH BETTER SOLDIER → 52%

. . . A SOMEWHAT BETTER SOLDIER → 37%

HAS NO EFFECT (5%) →
. . . A POORER SOLDIER (6%) →

LEADERSHIP MEANS LESS DEPRIVATION

Having a commander who has always done his best to look after his
soldiers' food, shelter and other comforts makes a man. . .

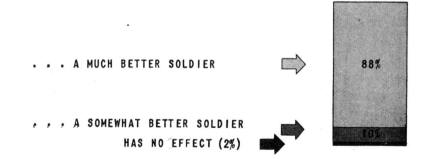

. . . A MUCH BETTER SOLDIER → 88%

. . . A SOMEWHAT BETTER SOLDIER
HAS NO EFFECT (2%) → 10%

Against fear . . .

LOYALTY AND PRIDE

Men take a kind of hard pride in belonging to a famous outfit even when doing so exposes them to exceptional danger. This is an essential element in the psychology of shock troops.

Pride in outfit is rooted in pride in self. It is one of the most reliable antagonists of fear.

Practically every informant emphasized that being a member of a distinguished outfit had made him a better soldier. Even when that outfit faced the grimmest tasks, the answer is still the same. Ninety-two per cent stated that being a member of an outfit selected for dangerous jobs made them better soldiers.

The wish not to let friends down is also a strong motive. Ninety-four per cent of the men stated that they were better soldiers because of the fear that if they showed weakness they would endanger the lives of their friends.

Here shame at endangering friends is pitted against fear of the dangers in battle.

Taken along with other factors, pride in outfit and loyalty to friends can play a real rôle in resisting fear.

MEN WHO ARE PROUD of being
SHOCK-TROOPS ARE BETTER SOLDIERS

QUESTION: . . "What was the effect on your behavior of being proud
of your outfit as the kind they picked when there was
a hard job to do?"

ANSWER . . .

PERCENTAGE ANSWERING

"MADE ME A MUCH BETTER SOLDIER" ⟹ 66%

"MADE ME A SOMEWHAT BETTER SOLDIER" ⟹ 26%

"HAD NO EFFECT" ⟹ 8%

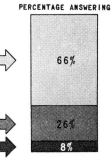

MEMBERSHIP IN A FAMOUS OUTFIT
TENDS TO MAKE MEN BETTER SOLDIERS

QUESTION. . . "What was the effect on your behavior of being a member of an outfit which had made a name for itself?"

ANSWER . . .

"MADE ME A MUCH BETTER SOLDIER" ⟹ 74%

"MADE ME A SOMEWHAT BETTER SOLDIER" ⟹ 23%

"HAD NO EFFECT"(3%) ⟹

HATRED AND ANGER

Hatred is necessary to the good fighter. Eighty-three per cent of our soldier informants emphasize this fact. Hatred distracts from fear and *also* motivates effective battle action.

But the comments of the men present an important qualification. The enemy soldier should be hated as a representative of the Fascist system, not as a mere personal ill-doer. Hatred of the enemy system can be a sustained, steady anger which lasts until the final battle is won.

Thinking of damage inflicted by the enemy on helpless civilians or of the bombing of cities by enemy planes helps make better soldiers, evidently by arousing hatred. This opinion is expressed by more than 80 per cent of the men.

Seeing a close friend killed brought a flare of anger which prompted to revenge in 79 per cent of the soldiers reporting. The death of a close friend is much more important in inciting anger than the sight of dead comrades whom one does not know; twice as many men reported being angry in the former case as in the latter.

While the immediate flash of anger and thirst for revenge is a useful motive in combatting fear, our informants are firm in the opinion that the long-time hatred excited by the symbols and agents of the Fascist cause is far more important.

DO MEN WHO HAVE a strong feeling of HATRED for the enemy . . .

. . . FIGHT MORE EFFECTIVELY?

ON THIS QUESTION. . .

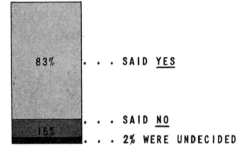

83% . . . SAID <u>YES</u>

15% . . . SAID <u>NO</u>

. . . 2% WERE UNDECIDED

REVENGE is a strong MOTIVE FOR FIGHTING

Our informants were asked: "What was the effect on your behavior as a soldier of wanting to get revenge after seeing a close friend killed?"

ON THIS QUESTION. . .

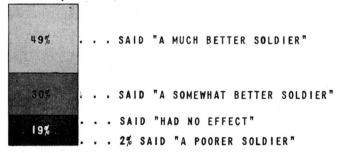

49% . . . SAID "A MUCH BETTER SOLDIER"

30% . . . SAID "A SOMEWHAT BETTER SOLDIER"

. . . SAID "HAD NO EFFECT"

19% . . . 2% SAID "A POORER SOLDIER"

MEN MAY FIGHT BETTER WHEN DANGER IS GREATER

Fear tends to weaken the attacking zeal of the soldier. But in some cases the stab of fear sets up thoughts which drive the soldier into action with greater than ordinary power.

Seventy-one per cent of the soldiers stated that there was an occasion when they had fought harder and better after overcoming great fear.

Their comment shows that even though afraid they began to think of their friends, of the outfit as a whole, of the cause which was at stake. These thoughts, following upon fear, actually made them more effective.

Such fear-resisting thoughts seem likely to occur when danger to the self also points to danger for the group. For example, some of the men had the experience of being sent in to plug a serious hole in the lines, and 64 per cent of them found it made them better soldiers. Such a gap in the lines means increased danger for the man but it also means that his outfit and, to some degree, his cause is in danger also. A similar number answer that they fought better in an "all-cost" action. The reasoning seems to be the same. An "all-cost" action, though dangerous, is one of great importance to the cause and challenges every soldier to do more than his best.

To respond in this way, however, the soldier must be strongly identified with his cause, must feel that its ultimate success matters greatly to him.

—AN ALL-COST ACTION

Four out of ten of the veterans had the experience of "Having to take a position at all costs."

Of those who took part in an all-cost action. . .

PERCENTAGE WHO BELIEVE IT MADE THEM. . .

. . . A BETTER SOLDIER

. . . NOT A BETTER SOLDIER

—PLUGGING A GAP IN THE LINES

Six out of ten had the experience of "being sent in to plug a serious hole in the lines."

Of those who had this experience. . .

PERCENTAGE WHO FELT IT MADE THEM. . .

. . . A BETTER SOLDIER

. . . NOT A BETTER SOLDIER

Against fear . . .

STRAIGHT NEWS about the WAR

The informed man is armed against lie and rumor. He is not expecting evil of the unfamiliar, is less likely to be distrustful of his remote superiors.

Eighty-nine per cent of these soldiers thought it better to give the men the straight news on the war, even when it was bad news. The men argued that if correct information is not given, the soldier will eventually find out the truth, but with the result that thenceforth all news from above will be discounted.

War news of immediate significance to the soldier is especially important.

He should understand the tactical importance of the objective which he is asked to take or hold. In this way his immediate daily behavior is related to the conduct of the war as a whole. If he wants to win, he can see himself as a factor in doing so. Ninety-five per cent of the men gave this opinion.

The men should understand the over-all political and military strategy of the war they fight. All of our informants stated that such knowledge makes a better soldier. To whatever extent possible the men should be linked to the total plan of the war, should feel that danger faced, work done, are part of a step-by-step progress toward final victory. Victory, they say, is won day-by-day by the informed soldier.

... AND KNOWLEDGE OF OBJECTIVES

QUESTION. . . "What was the effect on your behavior of knowing that you were getting straight news on what was happening on the whole front, even though the news may have been fairly bad?"

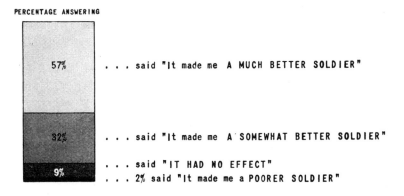

PERCENTAGE ANSWERING

57% . . . said "It made me A MUCH BETTER SOLDIER"

32% . . . said "It made me A SOMEWHAT BETTER SOLDIER"

9% . . . said "IT HAD NO EFFECT"
. . . 2% said "It made me a POORER SOLDIER"

QUESTION. . . "What was the effect on your behavior of knowing the strategic importance of your immediate objective. . . Why it was important to hold or take a particular position?"

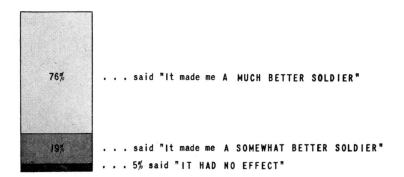

76% . . . said "It made me A MUCH BETTER SOLDIER"

19% . . . said "It made me A SOMEWHAT BETTER SOLDIER"
. . . 5% said "IT HAD NO EFFECT"

THE BEST KIND OF DISCIPLINE

Our men distinguish between voluntary discipline and formal discipline and vote overwhelmingly for the former.

Discipline is of course always imposed by a line of command but it makes a great difference, so these men think, whether the soldier understands why discipline is necessary and to what general end it is enforced. The ideally disciplined man is an instructed man. He knows what he is fighting for. He has accepted army discipline as a command of his own conscience.

Sixty per cent of the men agree that good discipline can be achieved by showing the man his personal stake in the war. Many stress that the qualities of officers have much to do with good discipline. They must be informed, capable and fair. Others in less numbers emphasize the importance of explaining the reasons for orders, the necessity for carrying out a particular act. A few think it helpful to relax formal discipline when not in battle.

Explaining to the men how discipline is useful in battle, how it saves lives, achieves results, is unanimously held to be important. Conversely, "training for automatic obedience by never explaining the reasons for commands" is believed by 89 per cent of the men to produce poorer soldiers.

This point has been emphasized many times. The willing soldier, the informed soldier, makes the best soldier.

THE WILLING SOLDIER
makes the BEST SOLDIER

"VOLUNTARY" DISCIPLINE. . .

95% favor the kind of inner discipline that exists when men understand the value of discipline. . . obey orders willingly. . . discipline themselves. . .and share responsibility for the discipline of their group.

"FORMAL" DISCIPLINE. . .

Only 5% favor the kind of discipline that results mainly from fear of punishment.

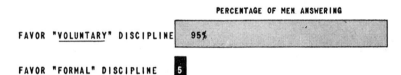

PERCENTAGE OF MEN ANSWERING

FAVOR "VOLUNTARY" DISCIPLINE   95%

FAVOR "FORMAL" DISCIPLINE   5

THE BEST SOLDIER knows . . .
. . . why DISCIPLINE IS NEEDED IN COMBAT

Explaining to men in training "how discipline is useful and why it is needed in combat" tends to make them. . .

PERCENTAGE ANSWERING

MUCH BETTER SOLDIERS   ➡   90%

SOMEWHAT BETTER SOLDIERS   ➡
HAS NO EFFECT (1%) ➡    9%

A FEAR POLICY FOR THE SOLDIER

Fear is a normal, inevitable, useful reaction to danger. It is a danger-signal produced in a man's body by his awareness of signs of danger in the world around him.

No man who is afraid in battle need be ashamed if his fear is under control. It is not fear that matters, but what a man does when he is afraid.

Controlled fear has the power to incite a man to useful action. Uncontrolled fear is destructive; it has the power to incite in a man a senseless panic which further endangers his life.

The objective of good fear policy is to manage fear. Fear should be rationed so that it never becomes too weak nor too strong. When fear is too weak a man gets reckless. When it is too strong he loses self-control; other men see his fear and become afraid.

Even though fear be very strong, a soldier can learn to manage it and keep it at a useful level. The fear of being known as a coward is a useful fear. Pitted against fear of battle, it can help a green man go through his first actions.

The veteran learns to distinguish between the real and unreal dangers of battle. He can learn also other techniques of controlling fear.

In order to use techniques of fear reduction, a soldier must be able to recognize fear before it becomes so strong that nothing can be done about it. Knowing the symptoms of fear, knowing where to expect danger, knowing the conditions under which fear adds up with other powerful motives makes it possible for a man to be on his guard against excessive fear.

Distraction of attention from danger, and concentration on the task at hand are important techniques for reducing fear. The use of these techniques is learned by experience and by sharing experience. Discussing the whole problem of fear with other soldiers is a way of learning from their experience.

But fear-reducing techniques are not always useful or possible. There are times, especially before battle, when a man is up against fear that comes from his own thoughts—his thoughts of the dangers he is going to meet. In battle itself there are times when fear has to be endured. Something more effective than fear-reducing techniques is needed.

The fundamental thing that controls a man's fear is an internal force which is stronger than his fear. Hatred for the enemy is such a force. Devotion to the Army and its leaders, pride in outfit, loyalty to friends, and, above all, feeling strongly about the war aims are the most powerful anti-fear forces. A man who has these forces in him can act intelligently and decisively *even when he is very much afraid*. Such a man has courage. Courage is not fearlessness; it is being able to do the job even when afraid.

A soldier with good training, intelligent leadership, and adequate equipment may be a good fighting man for a long time without caring about the things he is fighting for. But sooner or later he will face temporary defeat, hunger, fatigue, sickness, and evil rumor. In such a crisis he may go to pieces. The man who has loyalty to his cause, in addition to equipment and skill, can best stand this test.

A positive will to win may not be important when training, equipment, and overwhelming superiority in numbers are on the soldier's side. But when forces are equal, those soldiers win who most want to win.

PART V: FACTS ABOUT THE REPORT

RELIABILITY

The foregoing data were compiled from a 44-page questionnaire. The questionnaire itself was designed on the basis of 20 recorded interviews. The questionnaire included both free-answer and check-list type questions. In all, 300 veterans filled out the questionnaire.

The number of answers to any one question was usually less than 300; at least some men failed to answer any one question. Of the 199 questions asked on the questionnaire, the data on 62 questions were used in the report. In 41 of these 62 questions, the "no answer" category was 5 per cent or less. In 14 of the 62 questions, the "no answer" category was from 6 to 10 per cent in frequency. In three cases the "no answer" group fell in the 10 to 15 per cent category. In four additional questions the "no answer" category ran above 15 per cent.

The two extreme cases of these four will be discussed here. In the case of "Fears That Didn't Pan Out" (page 20), 130 men (43 per cent) made no response. In this case nothing was claimed for the rank order of the percentages of different fears because of this large "no answer" vote. The next most frequent "no answer," *i.e.,* 24 per cent, was obtained on the question on "Changes in Fear" (page 18). Examination revealed that this was an exceptionally difficult question for the men since it involved a system of ranking that they found intricate. The highest number of unsuccessful attempts at response was recorded for this question. It seems a fair assumption that the responses in this case represent the more intelligent men, or at least those most adept at responding to a poorly designed question. In the other two cases of "no answer" in excess of 15 per cent, only an extreme and highly improbable distribution of the missing answers would affect the rank orders as given.

Some informants selected themselves out of the sample by giving "no experience" votes to particular questions. This raises the question of the size of the actual "N's" used to compute percentages or determine rank orders. In 52 of the 62 cases, the actual "N's," *i.e.,* 300 minus both "no answer" and "no experience" votes, fell between 200 and 300. In ten cases the actual "N's" fell below 200. The latter cases have been carefully examined and differentially charted and reported in the text. As an example of the treatment of five of these items, see the charts on pages 44, 47 and 65, and appended text. When percentages or rank orders seemed unstable because of the small "N's" this fact has been reflected in the text.

The expression "of the men" has been used throughout, as in the case "90 per cent *of the men* felt thus-and-so." This seemed clearer and less confusing than to keep stressing that such-and-such a percentage "of the men *who answered*" felt in a certain way.

An inevitable defect of the sample arose from the fact that we could not select informants by lot. Many of the veterans were at sea as merchant seamen; a large number were in the United States Army. Both of these groups were inaccessible. Only 300 informants could be obtained. But there has appeared no good evidence that the veterans who were not accessible were different in any systematic way from those who were. We conclude that the opinions expressed in our present sample are representative for the group as a whole.

VALIDITY

Since the object of the research is to offer data which may be useful to the authorities in the American Army concerned with the fear problem, the question arises as to whether these findings could be transferred from the sample at hand to a similar sample of troops in the Army of the United States. This matter could be finally determined only by a parallel study of American troops after they had spent a period of time in combat. For the moment, some considerations can be offered for and against the assumption that one can predict from this sample to troops in the American Army. *Against* the possibility of prediction, the following considerations must be offered:

1. Members of the Abraham Lincoln Brigade were exclusively volunteers. A relatively small percentage of the men in the American Army are volunteers. It is possible that these findings could be paralleled more closely in a study of the specialized volunteer services like the Air Corps, Marines, or Paratroopers, than in the body of American troops.

2. Many, perhaps most, of the A.L.B. veterans had a strong sense of "cause." They viewed the struggle in Spain as a first step in the war against Fascism and for the democratic forces of the world. Only U. S. Army specialists on morale can answer the question as to whether our men are similarly motivated.

3. They were fighting in a technically inferior army. We may suppose that as to training, organization and matériel they were undoubtedly inferior to our own well-organized army.

4. Although occasionally victorious, the A.L.B. also suffered de-

feats and retreats, and heavy casualties were inflicted on them. Despite such adverse conditions, they fought well.

5. The A.L.B. veterans were largely men from big cities. Nine out of ten came from cities of a hundred thousand or over. This fact about the sample must differentiate it from the composition of the American Army as a whole.

In *favor* of the possibility of predicting from this sample are these considerations:

1. Fear in the face of danger is presumably a common human emotion. There is no reason to think that one group of men would be less distinguished by it than another.

2. Testimony of the A.L.B. veterans seems to be sensible. They admit fear and have practical suggestions for combatting it.

3. The fundamentals of modern war are presumably alike everywhere. Soldiers in different armies must therefore acquire a common fund of experience. Some of this experience should be transferable from one army to another regardless of differences in cause, composition, or other circumstances.

4. This sample is composed of very experienced men from a military standpoint. Seventy-four per cent of them had more than six months front-line experience, and fifty-eight per cent had been wounded at least once. Such protracted front-line experience should have taught them the lessons of battle and given them a fund of experience to impart.

Each person concerned to apply the results of this study must judge for himself the likelihood that the findings will be transferable.

ERRORS OF REPORT

There are some possible errors which do not concern statistical reliability or transferability to another army organization. These may be called errors of reporting. Questionnaires present certain stimuli to respondents. These stimuli take the form of sentences, questions, and the like. The respondent is required to produce a sentence in return. The respondent's sentences have presumably been formulated in some exacting situation of experience—in this case, the danger experiences of battle. The question then arises: Are the sentences that he produces now the same ones that he formulated in the face of the actual situation? Certainly, we should point out that sentences have a tendency to fade. They are more accurate when produced nearer to the situation to which they are appropriate. For instance, some of the 26 per cent of our veterans who reported that they were not afraid in their first action may have "forgotten" their fear.

Sentences also have a tendency to get borrowed. Men talk over their experiences after battle and some may be more persuasive than others in getting their views adopted. There is no way to estimate correctly the likelihood that this borrowing has occurred in the present case, but there is some evidence to indicate that it did occur to a degree. Then again, there might be a tendency to idealize "the past," that is, to change the sentences formed on the spot in a direction which would present the informant in a better light. Since the data provided by our questionnaire seem to check well with the newspaper accounts of the time and the books subsequently produced by members of the Brigade, we believe that our data have not been idealized.

CAUSE AND IDENTIFICATION
WITH CAUSE

Identification with cause is a psychological process; the cause itself is an ideological system. Causes may possibly be ranked according to the degree to which they permit identification throughout a society as a whole. For instance, "defending the homeland" as a cause would be readily intelligible for the masses of men; whereas, many men might lack the technical information and understanding of seemingly remote dangers required to give content to the "Four Freedoms." "Asia for Asiatics" as a race cry may permit relatively ready identification; whereas, "fight against encirclement" may be intelligible to a much more limited section of the population. The problem of producing identification with cause, then, is not merely a matter of working the information machinery properly; it depends in some part on the cause in which belief is to be produced. Some causes have an immediate impact throughout every level in a society. Others require a degree of technical information which limits the number of men who can experience a strong identification. Quite apart from the "pull" of the cause itself is the question of the excellence of the informational and educational machinery which fosters identification.

When educative techniques are efficient, they serve to produce that degree of mass identification with the particular cause which is inherently possible.

[63]

CONCERNING UNCONSCIOUS FEAR

It was not possible in this report to get an adequate description of the premilitary personality of the informant or to estimate different degrees of unconscious fear which the men brought into battle. The report, therefore, does not treat differences between unconscious and conscious fear. Unconscious fears of civilian life are undoubtedly transferred to the danger situations of battle. Men are in many cases more afraid than these dangers would actually justify, bad as they may sometimes be. Those who panic or develop neurosis under battle conditions may well be those in whom an exceptional degree of civilian fear was added to the fears normal under battle conditions. Nothing in our evidence serves to challenge this proposition. The questionnaire situation, however, does not offer an opportunity to distinguish between the rational and irrational fears of battle. Their consideration was perforce left to one side. It might be noted that there was no attempt to "screen" the volunteers of the A.L.B. from the psychiatric standpoint. There is no reason to believe that they did not have normal levels of unconscious fear. The fact that this fear seems to have been kept quite well in check by their very positive stand on the ideological issues of the war may be an important bit of testimony.